VOICING DISSENT

The Power and Pitfalls of Student Protests

Carla Mooney

San Diego, CA

About the Author

Carla Mooney is the author of many books for young adults and children. She lives in Pittsburgh, Pennsylvania, with her husband and three children.

© 2025 ReferencePoint Press, Inc.
Printed in the United States

For more information, contact:
ReferencePoint Press, Inc.
PO Box 27779
San Diego, CA 92198
www.ReferencePointPress.com

ALL RIGHTS RESERVED.
No part of this work covered by the copyright hereon may be reproduced or used in any form or by any means—graphic, electronic, or mechanical, including photocopying, recording, taping, web distribution, or information storage retrieval systems—without the written permission of the publisher.

Picture Credits:
Cover: Ringo Chiu/Shutterstock

 5: Sipa USA via AP
 9: Ian Dagnall/Alamy Stock Photo
13: Science History Images/Alamy Stock Photo
16: Bridgeman Images
19: Associated Press
22: John Sohm/Visions of American/Newscom
24: Liv Oeian/Shutterstock
30: L Paul Mann/Shutterstock
32: Tribune Content Agency LLC/Alamy Stock Photo
34: Associated Press
39: Associated Press
42: Galsshouse Images/Newscom
46: Robyn Stevens Brody/Sipa USA/Newscom
49: Sheila Fitzgerald/Shutterstock
51: BearFotos/Shutterstock
55: Avpics/Alamy Stock Photo

LIBRARY OF CONGRESS CATALOGING-IN-PUBLICATION DATA

Names: Mooney, Carla, 1970- author.
Title: Voicing dissent : the power and pitfalls of student protests / By Carla Mooney.
Description: San Diego, CA : ReferencePoint Press, [2024] | Includes bibliographical references and index.
Identifiers: LCCN 2024044667 (print) | LCCN 2024044668 (ebook) | ISBN 9781678210168 (library binding) | ISBN 9781678210175 (ebook)
Subjects: LCSH: Students--Political activity--United States--Juvenile literature. | Student movements--United States--Juvenile literature. | Youth movements--United States--Juvenile literature.
Classification: LCC LB3610 .M66 2024 (print) | LCC LB3610 (ebook) | DDC 371.8/10973--dc23
LC record available at https://lccn.loc.gov/2024044667
LC ebook record available at https://lccn.loc.gov/2024044668

CONTENTS

Introduction   4
Protests at Columbia University

Chapter One   8
The Importance of Public Protest

Chapter Two   18
The Power of Student Protests

Chapter Three   28
Protest Pitfalls and Backlash

Chapter Four   38
Vandalism and Violence on Campus

Chapter Five   48
The Future of Student Protests

Source Notes   57
For Further Research   61
Index   63

INTRODUCTION

Protests at Columbia University

Near dawn on April 17, 2024, hundreds of college students set up nearly sixty tents on Columbia University's South Lawn. The students rallied to speak out against the Israel-Hamas War, which broke out after the Hamas terrorist group killed and kidnapped hundreds of Israeli citizens on October 7, 2023. The world was outraged by the initial attack on Israel. However, months into the war, many people, including students, were horrified by the war's large number of civilian casualties in Gaza, the territory that has been home to about 2.1 million Palestinians. Protesters said they believed Israel's response to the Hamas attack had become a form of genocide against the Palestinian people.

In reaction, the students created the Gaza Solidarity Encampment in the middle of Columbia's campus. They displayed handwritten signs throughout the encampment with slogans calling for the university to sever any financial ties to Israel. Chants of "Free, free Palestine!"[1] rang out throughout the encampment. The students pledged to occupy the campus lawn until the university complied.

Swift Reaction

By noon on April 17, Columbia's administrators informed protesting students that their encampment violated the school's policies and presented a safety concern. Administrators warned students that they could face academic sanctions if they did not leave the lawn and gave them a deadline of 9:00 p.m. to depart. However, the protesters refused.

On April 18 Columbia University president Minouche Shafik asked the New York Police Department (NYPD) for help clearing the protesters and their tents from campus. "The individuals who established the encampment violated a long list of rules and policies,"[2] says Shafik. According to Shafik, university officials had been unsuccessful in discussions with the protesters but had offered to continue discussions if the protesters agreed to remove the encampment. When the protesters refused, police dressed in riot gear cleared the lawn, arrested more than one hundred protesters for trespassing, and removed the tent encampment. "Students have the right to free speech but do not have the right to violate university policies and disrupt learning on campus,"[3] said New York City mayor Eric Adams.

> "Students have the right to free speech but do not have the right to violate university policies and disrupt learning on campus."[3]
>
> —Eric Adams, New York City mayor

The Final Clash

The police involvement only inflamed the protesters. The next day students and outsiders returned to the lawn. Within days they

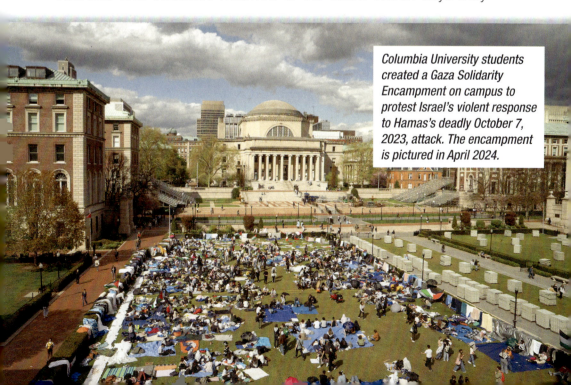

Columbia University students created a Gaza Solidarity Encampment on campus to protest Israel's violent response to Hamas's deadly October 7, 2023, attack. The encampment is pictured in April 2024.

had set up the tents again without Columbia's permission. As the protests continued, university officials attempted to negotiate with the protesters. Concerned with student safety, the university restricted access to its campus and canceled in-person classes, forcing all students to finish the semester via remote learning.

On April 30 dozens of protesters took over the university's Hamilton Hall. They barricaded the building's entrances and hung a Free Palestine banner from a window. The student protesters insisted they would not leave the building until Columbia met their demands: divest from Israeli companies, agree to be transparent with university investments, and grant amnesty to the protesters. Once again, university administrators called NYPD officers to campus. Hundreds of police officers carrying riot shields stormed Hamilton Hall. They arrested more than one hundred protesters and loaded them onto large buses. Later that night Columbia employees began to take down the tents, and by the following day, the campus lawn was empty. Citing safety concerns, university officials later canceled the schoolwide commencement ceremony.

Concerns of Other Students

For some students at Columbia, the atmosphere around the encampment grew increasingly hostile. In some cases, the pro-Palestinian demonstrations turned into harassment of Columbia's Jewish students. Some protesters who were not affiliated with the university launched a series of verbal attacks on Jewish students, leaving them afraid for their safety on campus. Chabad, a Jewish organization at Columbia, issued a statement claiming that some protesters had yelled profanities at Jewish students as they walked through campus and told them to leave America and return to Europe. One student reported that protesters stole an Israeli flag and tried to burn it.

In response to the increasing tension, Samantha Slater, a Columbia spokesperson, issued a statement emphasizing that the university was committed to ensuring that all students remained safe on campus. "Columbia students have the right to protest, but they are not allowed to disrupt campus life or harass and intimidate fellow students and members of our community. We are acting on concerns we are hearing from our Jewish students and are providing additional support and resources to ensure that our community remains safe,"[4] she said in the statement.

Supporting Causes and Concerns

Student protests have a long history in the United States. Over the years, many students have protested in support of various causes, often reflecting the time's social, political, and economic concerns. In the 1950s equal rights protests occurred in cities nationwide as Black citizens spoke out for their rights and equal treatment. In the 1960s antiwar protests surged in response to the Vietnam War. In recent years students have organized protests around racial justice, sexual assault, climate change, gun control and Second Amendment rights, student loan debt, and other issues.

In many cases protest can be a powerful tool that students can use to voice dissent. Protests can spotlight issues, get the mainstream public's attention, and provide a platform for marginalized communities to get the recognition necessary to bring about meaningful change. "Public opinion changes on the issues as a result of the effectiveness of the protests doing one very important thing, raising the visibility and salience of the issues,"[5] says Robert Shapiro, professor of political science at Columbia University. However, students must balance the power of protests with potential drawbacks. Sometimes, protest activities can infringe on the rights of others or lead to students facing disciplinary action from schools or possibly arrest. Some protests have even escalated into harassment and violence, which can detract from the very issues protesters want to highlight.

> "Public opinion changes on the issues as a result of the effectiveness of the protests doing one very important thing, raising the visibility and salience of the issues."[5]
>
> —Robert Shapiro, professor of political science at Columbia University

CHAPTER ONE

The Importance of Public Protest

The United States has a long history of protest and free expression. Protest movements have led to many important reforms in the United States, including abolishing slavery and ensuring voting rights for women. Through peaceful assembly and protest, Americans can express their opinions on important issues and have a voice in shaping American society.

Protest: A Constitutional Right

At the founding of the United States, American colonists treasured the rights of private citizens. Before the American Revolution, the colonists were under the rule of the British king and Parliament. After the colonists fought for and gained independence from Britain, they were determined to protect the rights of citizens from authorities like the king.

The Founding Fathers carefully constructed a new American government that protected individual rights. They protected the right to free expression in the First Amendment to the US Constitution, which prohibited the federal government from restricting people's right to express their opinions or peacefully protest government policies. The First Amendment states, "Congress shall make no law respecting an establishment of religion, or prohibiting the free exercise thereof; or abridging the freedom of speech, or of the press; or the right of the people peaceably to assemble, and to petition the Government for a redress of grievances."[6]

The rights guaranteed in the Constitution's First Amendment form the cornerstone for every citizen's right to gather and participate in peaceful protests. The right to free expression is a core principle of a democracy. When people support or oppose a policy, they can speak out without fear of being silenced by the government. They can try to convince others to agree with their viewpoint and build a majority that can change policies or laws. Without the right to free expression, the government could prevent citizens from objecting to its policies and laws and even stop them from publicly talking negatively about the government. Although the First Amendment initially only applied to the federal government, later amendments and court decisions have broadened it to apply to state governments.

A Few Limits

Although Americans have the right to express themselves freely, there are a few limitations. Some types of speech are not protected under the First Amendment. The government can ban speech that includes defamation, fraud, obscenity, incitement of violence, speech integral to criminal conduct, genuine threats, and child

George Washington (standing, right) speaks at the signing of the US Constitution in 1787. By 1791, three-fourths of the states had ratified the ten amendments that became known as the Bill of Rights.

> "Universities can limit the time, place and manner of protests, as long as those limits aren't intended to stop the protest entirely and are applied to all viewpoints equally."[8]
>
> —Kevin Goldberg, First Amendment specialist at the Freedom Forum

pornography. Also, the First Amendment only applies to government actions and does not guarantee a person's right to free speech without consequences in a private forum. Legal scholars Geoffrey Stone and Eugene Volokh explain, "The First Amendment does not protect speakers . . . against private individuals or organizations, such as private employers, private colleges, or private landowners. The First Amendment restrains only the government."[7]

The government can also place some reasonable restrictions on the time, place, and manner of public assemblies. For example, the government can limit noise levels, establish a maximum number of protests or people that can occupy an area, prevent early-morning or late-night protests, and restrict the size or placement of signs on government property. Some local areas require protesters to obtain parade or demonstration permits.

The First Amendment on Campus

Public universities receive funding from the government, which places them under the same First Amendment and constitutional rules as public lands. Therefore, on public university campuses, students can express their views and participate in protests if they do not break any laws or incite violence. "Universities can limit the time, place and manner of protests, as long as those limits aren't intended to stop the protest entirely and are applied to all viewpoints equally,"[8] writes Kevin Goldberg, the First Amendment specialist at the Freedom Forum, a foundation dedicated to protecting First Amendment freedoms.

In comparison, private colleges and universities are not bound by the First Amendment. They are free to establish policies and codes of conduct that limit student speech and behavior. Ben Wizner, a director at the American Civil Liberties Union, says:

Unless there is a relevant state law, private colleges and universities can have whatever protest policies they want, including prohibiting all protests if that's their decision. Now, most private colleges adopt free expression principles that at least approximate the standards of the First Amendment. But it's important to know that those are not generally enforceable. So if they decide that they don't like the direction of a particular protest movement, they can change those rules.[9]

A Long History of Student Activism

On public and private school campuses, students have exercised their right to speak out on the issues they are passionate about for many decades. One of the first waves of student activism occurred in the late 1920s and the 1930s. After the New York Stock Exchange crashed in 1929, the value of company stocks fell dramatically, and the country entered the Great Depression. Businesses failed, and many workers lost their jobs. By 1932 one of

Civil Disobedience

Civil disobedience has a long history in the United States. Civil disobedience is a protest in which individuals intentionally refuse to follow specific laws. Nonviolent civil disobedience has often been used to demand social change. One of the earliest examples of American civil disobedience occurred in 1773 when Boston colonists broke the law by throwing tea into Boston Harbor to protest taxes the British had imposed on the colonies. A key component of civil disobedience is that it remains nonviolent. Protesters are not breaking laws that ban violence. They do not use weapons or put the lives or safety of others at risk. Instead, protesters break discriminatory laws or those that block organized protests. "Those who engage in civil disobedience demonstrate the sincerity of their protests and their respect for the rule of law and fundamental democratic principles by not resisting the force of the law, remaining non-violent, and accepting the legal penalty for their actions," writes philosopher Peter Singer. On campus, civil disobedience often takes the form of erecting tent encampments or occupying buildings or other campus spaces without permission.

Quoted in Lawrence Torcello, "Campus Protests Are Part of an Enduring Legacy of Civil Disobedience Improving American Democracy," The Conversation, May 22, 2024. https://theconversation.com.

every four US workers was unemployed. As the country's banks failed, many Americans lost their savings. Without savings or jobs, some lost their homes and struggled to feed their families.

Students joined other citizens in demonstrations, marches, and hunger strikes nationwide to protest the country's economic situation. Protesters called for relief funds to help the unemployed facing hunger, eviction, and homelessness. In 1932 the country elected Franklin D. Roosevelt as president. Seeing the widespread protests and recognizing the people's unrest, Roosevelt's administration responded. It implemented many relief programs, including several programs that created desperately needed jobs for the unemployed.

Sit-In Movement for Civil Rights

Students made a memorable stand for equal rights during the civil rights movement in the 1960s. In February 1960 four Black students from North Carolina A&T State University walked into a Greensboro, North Carolina, department store and sat down at a Whites-only lunch counter. The students had planned this action for weeks to protest the city's segregation laws. In many southern communities, local laws existed to separate where Black and White people could live, work, eat, and shop. Although the waitress denied service to the students, they calmly refused to leave. The police were called but did not arrest the students, since their "sit-in" protest was not violent. The students remained in their seats until the lunch counter closed. The next day, more students sat at the lunch counter. This time, the sit-in attracted the attention of local media.

The sit-in protests quickly spread to other colleges, inspiring thousands of Black and White college students to join the civil rights movement. By the end of February, students had held sit-ins at more than thirty locations across seven states. By the end of April, more than fifty thousand students had participated in sit-in protests. According to civil rights activist Martin Luther King Jr.,

In February 1960, Black students sit at a Whites-only lunch counter in Charlotte, North Carolina. Students in other cities did the same to protest segregation laws and demand equal rights.

the sit-ins were an "electrifying movement . . . [that] shattered the placid surface of campuses and communities across the South."[10]

Nonviolence was a key component of the student-led sit-ins, even when protesters faced heckling, assault, and arrest. King applauded the students' determination to remain peaceful in their protest. He wrote, "The key significance of the student movement lies in the fact that from its inception, everywhere, it has combined direct action with non-violence. This quality has given it the extraordinary power and discipline which every thinking person observes."[11]

Eventually, these student-led sit-in protests prompted many places to change their segregation policies. They also led to the formation of student groups to coordinate civil rights actions. Some student activists who participated in sit-ins formed the Student Nonviolent Coordinating Committee in 1960. Their activism, which emphasized peaceful and direct-action protests, had a significant role in the civil rights movement.

> "The key significance of the student movement lies in the fact that from its inception, everywhere, it has combined direct action with non-violence."[11]
>
> —Martin Luther King Jr., civil rights activist

Free Speech Movement

Another notable student protest movement began at the University of California, Berkeley, in the 1960s. At the time, anti-Communist feelings were high in the United States, and California public universities passed several regulations limiting students' political activities and speech. At Berkeley, administrators banned students from participating in political activities, on or off campus.

However, the growing civil rights movement and anti–Vietnam War sentiment led students to disregard the bans. At first, students participated in off-campus protests, and university administrators ignored their activities. But when hundreds of Berkeley students were arrested at various off-campus protests, state legislators pressured the university to enforce its political activity bans. In response, Berkeley administrators issued orders to remind students not to participate in off-campus political activities.

In 1964 nearly five hundred Berkeley students marched on the university's administration building to protest the order. Student leaders called for an organized protest to push all schools

Earth Day

Students' energy and enthusiasm helped create the first Earth Day in 1970. Before that time, many Americans did not realize the effect of pollution on the environment and human health. In 1969, 3 million gallons (11.4 million L) of oil leaked off the California coast near Santa Barbara. It was one of the largest oil spills in US history. Oil covered 30 square miles (77.7 sq. km) of ocean, killing birds, sea lions, and other marine life. Senator Gaylord Nelson of Wisconsin recognized the energy of antiwar student protesters and believed the students' passions could be focused on environmental and pollution issues. He helped organize antipollution teach-ins, rallies, and demonstrations on college campuses nationwide. On April 22, 1970, nearly 20 million Americans, many of them college students, participated in the first Earth Day. Many of the students went on to form environmental clubs at their schools. "That brought about a movement that I think has been sustained on campuses across the country, and globally now to some extent," says Will Callaway, the national campaign director for Earth Day Network.

Quoted in Christi-Anne Weatherly, "Earth Day: It All Began with College Students," University of Florida Office of Sustainability, April 10, 2020. https://sustainable.ufl.edu.

in the University of California system to abandon all restrictions on students' free speech and assembly rights. The Free Speech Movement (FSM) was started at Berkeley.

On the Berkeley campus, students organized several smaller sit-ins and demonstrations that swelled into large rallies and protests. Students called on the university to ditch its restrictions on free speech and follow the guidelines established by the First Amendment, particularly for expressions of political views. Eventually, pressure from the FSM led the university to remove its policies restricting free speech. "The Free Speech Movement was the first revolt of the 1960s to bring to a college campus the mass civil disobedience tactics pioneered in the civil rights movement. Those tactics, most notably the sit-in, would give students unprecedented leverage to make demands on university administrators, setting the stage for mass student protests against the Vietnam War,"[12] writes Robert Cohen, author of *Freedom's Orator*.

Opposition to the Vietnam War

In the 1950s a long, costly conflict began in Southeast Asia between the Communist country of North Vietnam and its neighbor, South Vietnam. As one of South Vietnam's allies, the United States became involved in the conflict. The United States and other democratic countries feared that a victory for North Vietnam would further spread communism throughout Asia. As US involvement in the Vietnam conflict increased in the 1960s, antiwar views in the United States also intensified. Students in particular opposed the war, and it became the center of many student protests nationwide.

On campuses nationwide, student groups held antiwar protests and demonstrations. At some schools, faculty who also opposed the war held teach-ins. At the University of Michigan in Ann Arbor, two hundred faculty held a teach-in by canceling classes and holding antiwar seminars. This form of protest spread quickly

Despite a strong police presence, young demonstrators protest the Vietnam War with a sit-in. This event, which took place in Washington, DC, in 1972, was one of many protests organized by student groups to speak against the war.

to other campuses. Some teach-ins had lectures and discussions. Others combined lectures with actions, such as antiwar protest marches.

As more young Americans were drafted into the military and sent into war, protests grew. Students held sit-ins and took over administration offices to protest the military draft. They burned draft cards and chanted antiwar slogans. Some protests were peaceful, but others turned violent. In 1970 an antiwar protest at Kent State University in Ohio turned tragic when members of the National Guard fired on protesting students, killing four and wounding nine others.

Raising Awareness

The work of previous students has laid the groundwork for modern student activists. Students past and present have employed several nonviolent tactics to raise awareness about issues. In many cases these tactics have effectively influenced public opinion and brought about change. Students peacefully occupy campus spaces to bring attention to important causes. They organize educational workshops and forums to discuss issues. They invite speakers and host debates to educate participants and encourage them to act on important issues.

Students also organize and participate in visible marches, rallies, and walkouts. These events provide a visual reminder to the public about issues of importance and show the unity of participants. Online, students create and use social media campaigns to inform others, spread their message, gather and mobilize supporters, and create a community that shares a common goal. With the power of the internet, students spread information quickly and widely, which often leads to greater participation and visibility for their causes.

Throughout American history, students and faculty at colleges and universities have fiercely defended their right to think and speak freely on issues that are important to them. This tradition of student protest upholds the First Amendment freedoms of speech, press, assembly, and petition. As the country's Founding Fathers recognized when they preserved these rights in the First Amendment, a healthy democracy depends on the ability of its citizens to hold leaders and those with power accountable for their actions. The Reverend F. Willis Johnson Jr., vice president of the Bridge Alliance, a nonprofit dedicated to building a healthy democracy, says:

> Our nation's Founding Fathers intentionally crafted the First Amendment with broad protections for unpopular speech and dissenting views to safeguard the republic's health. It is a bulwark against tyranny, and its protection of protest and assembly is essential to a functioning democracy. Protest inherently possesses an ability to mobilize public opinion and raise the bars of accountability and conscience, while injecting hope and optimism into public discourse.[13]

CHAPTER TWO

The Power of Student Protests

On October 13, 2014, hundreds of demonstrators gathered in St. Louis, Missouri. The protesters, including students and non-students, massed for a rally in the city's Shaw neighborhood, near the site where police had fatally shot a Black teenager, eighteen-year-old VonDerrit Myers Jr., after Myers allegedly shot at officers. Myers's death on October 8 sparked renewed frustration with law enforcement's treatment of young Black men. A few months earlier, in nearby Ferguson, Missouri, police had fatally shot Michael Brown, another Black teen.

Protesters marched through the city's downtown and headed toward Saint Louis University. Upon reaching campus in the early morning, the protesters gathered around the university clock tower. They announced plans to stay. "We are here to destroy systematic racism and white supremacy. This is a sit-in,"[14] said one protester.

A small group of protesters set up tents near the clock tower. Protesters held a sit-in for six days with daily teach-ins and community conversations. Students, faculty, and community members discussed race, equality, and poverty. The peaceful protest led to an agreement between students and university administrators to commit to several initiatives, known as the Clock Tower Accords. In the agreement, the university committed to actively strengthening diversity, inclusion, and equity on campus through various short- and long-term initiatives. At the end of the protest, university president Fred Pestello issued a letter to the St. Louis community.

"Now, the University must come together. We will move to more formal and institutionalized conversations about race on our campus. We also will begin to devise short- and long-term initiatives that retain and attract more students and faculty of color, promote equal opportunity, and advance focused economic development in disadvantaged neighborhoods,"[15] he stated.

Pestello thanked the university students for inspiring many by speaking out peacefully about their beliefs. "Spurring us on toward the peaceful outcome we have achieved this afternoon have been the many thoughtful and inspiring voices I have heard this week, especially from our students. Their commitment to our mission and values continues to inspire me each day,"[16] he said.

Mobilizing Student Protests

As the success in St. Louis demonstrates, student protests can be an effective way to raise awareness and show support for important issues. Protest activities unite people and make them feel part of a larger community and movement. Students have

Hundreds of demonstrators gather around the Saint Louis University clock tower in October 2014. They were protesting the recent shootings of two young Black men by police and demanding an end to systemic racism.

successfully held peaceful protests, from sit-ins and walkouts to rallies and boycotts. No matter the format, by working together, protesters join voices and efforts to influence others and inspire change in their communities.

In some cases student protests grow from grassroots efforts. A grassroots movement is an organized effort by ordinary people in a geographic area to bring about changes in policy or politics. The March for Our Lives event is an example of a grassroots student effort that grew into a national protest movement. On February 14, 2018, nineteen-year-old Nikolas Cruz walked into Marjory Stoneman Douglas High School in Parkland, Florida, armed with a semiautomatic rifle. Cruz, a former student at the public school, opened fire and killed seventeen students and staff. The horrific event was one more in a series of shootings impacting US schools over the past few decades.

The day after the shooting, Parkland survivor Cameron Kasky, an eleventh-grade student at the school, invited classmates Alex Wind and Jaclyn Corin to his house. Together, they began plan-

Buildings Renamed

In June 2020 students at James Madison University (JMU) in Harrisonburg, Virginia, led a silent march through campus. Joined by university employees and community members, the JMU students marched from one end of campus to the other. The first eight minutes and forty-six seconds were held in silence in remembrance of George Floyd, a Black man who died in May 2020 after a Minneapolis police officer knelt on his neck for that length of time. The students called for JMU to improve its efforts to fight systemic racism and to rename three buildings that had been named after Confederate leaders and slave owners. At the march, student leaders took turns speaking to the crowd. "We need to start focusing on pushing JMU to challenge the status quo," said Daerenz Lyons, one of the student leaders. "Right now is a time for action, and our action today is marching." Within a week, JMU president Jonathan Alger announced that he was recommending the removal of Confederate names from campus buildings. In July 2020 the university's governing board approved the name change for three buildings.

Quoted in Sukainah Abid-Kons, "JMU Students Lead Silent March to Turn Up Volume on Calls to End Systemic Racism and Remove Confederates' Names from Buildings," The Citizen, June 15, 2020. https://hburgcitizen.com.

ning a march for gun reform and started the #NeverAgain hashtag on Twitter. In the following days, Parkland students called for gun reform and publicly shamed political leaders whom they blamed for the nation's lenient gun laws. They did media interviews and wrote op-eds for news outlets. In an op-ed for CNN, Kasky wrote:

> We can't ignore the issues of gun control that this tragedy raises. And so, I'm asking—no, demanding—we take action now. Why? Because at the end of the day, the students at my school felt one shared experience—our politicians abandoned us by failing to keep guns out of schools. But this time, my classmates and I are going to hold them to account. This time, we are going to pressure them to take action.[17]

The Impact of Grassroots Campaigns

The students' voices and calls for change quickly went viral. Students called for specific gun reforms, including an assault weapons ban, universal background checks, and digital gun ownership records. In the process, the students started one of the most powerful grassroots gun reform movements in decades. They also announced plans for a protest rally and march in Washington, DC, on March 24 and invited students across the country to join them.

The students raised over $3.7 million in a few days for the event called March for Our Lives. The funds paid for the supplies, equipment, and coordination of the March 24 event. Partner organizations joined the students to provide transportation, housing, entertainment, food, and other resources for the event. For those who could not attend, the students prepared a tool kit to help other students organize their own marches.

On March 24 hundreds of thousands of students, parents, teachers, and victims rallied and marched in Washington, DC, and in cities nationwide to call for gun control measures. In DC, student speakers took the stage, including survivors of the Parkland

After the deadly 2018 high school shooting in Parkland, Florida, student survivors organized nationwide protests for new gun laws. This March for Our Lives rally in 2018 drew hundreds of thousands of supporters to Washington, DC.

shooting. They called for a ban on assault weapons, limits on high-capacity gun magazines, and universal background checks. They also urged the crowd to register to vote so they could elect leaders who would act on gun control. Up to 2 million people participated in rallies nationwide, making it one of the largest student-led protests in the United States since the Vietnam War.

Since 2018 student-led protests have impacted people and communities throughout America. March for Our Lives has grown from a single event to a youth-led movement to eliminate gun violence. In the years since the first march, the movement has helped pass more than three hundred gun violence prevention laws across the United States. In 2022 the Bipartisan Safer Communities Act, which was hailed as one of the most significant and comprehensive federal gun safety laws in decades, was passed by Congress and signed into law by President Joe Biden. On the second anniversary of the act's passage, Natalie Fall, the executive director of March for Our Lives, celebrated its achievements:

> Young people are safer today because of the Bipartisan Safer Communities Act, that's a fact. We can't know the precise number of lives saved, but we have an idea, and it should give us hope for progress in the fight against the gun violence epidemic. This is a historic achievement, and wouldn't have been possible without the relentless efforts of young people who took to the streets with March For Our Lives, and took their demands directly to the halls of power.[18]

A Powerful Impact

Student protests can have a powerful impact. Protests can spotlight the issues and causes that students support. By getting people's attention, protesters have the potential to influence public opinion, drive social change, and reform policies from the local to national to international level. "Student protests have been a catalyst for many of the most important reforms in American history,"[19] says protest historian Steven Mintz of the University of Texas at Austin.

The power of protest was demonstrated by a young Swedish schoolgirl named Greta Thunberg in 2018. In August, fifteen-year-old Thunberg sat outside the Swedish parliament building every school day for three weeks, holding signs to urge Swedish lawmakers to address the climate crisis. Before long, other students, parents, and teachers joined Thunberg's protest. In September Thunberg began to strike from school every Friday to protest climate issues. She created the hashtag #FridaysforFuture and invited students worldwide to join her for the weekly climate strikes. The movement quickly gained followers online, and by March 2019 more than 2 million people in 135 countries worldwide were

> "Student protests have been a catalyst for many of the most important reforms in American history."[19]
>
> —Steven Mintz, historian at the University of Texas at Austin

Greta Thunberg of Sweden (pictured in 2023) gained global recognition when she began her climate protests at age fifteen. Her actions have shown how a single student can inspire change.

participating in school climate strikes. With all the publicity for her climate cause, Thunberg wrote on Twitter, "Now I am speaking to the whole world."[20]

> "Now I am speaking to the whole world."[20]
>
> —Greta Thunberg, teen climate activist

Thunberg's actions showed how a single student can have a massive impact and inspire change in others. The student-led strikes renewed awareness of climate change. With more people focused on the problem, the student-led movement also drove social change and impacted public opinion in many ways, both large and small. Ishan Bipin Ajmera, a postdoctoral researcher at the University of Natural Resources and Life Sciences in Vienna, Austria, has seen how climate strikes have impacted people where he lives. "It seems that the climate protests have effectively raised awareness and influenced the public discourse on climate issues,"[21] he says.

A 2023 study supports the claim that climate strikes drive social change, sparking people to change their daily habits. The study, sponsored by the Swiss Federal Institute of Technology Lausanne, studied the impact of climate strikes on people's daily environmental choices. They found that almost one-third of Swiss people had changed their recycling, transportation, and buying habits because of the climate protests. People began walking or cycling to work instead of driving, eating more vegetarian meals, and making more effort to reduce plastic waste. "Our study found that this type of civic engagement through collective action can have a direct effect on society, confirming that such action is warranted," says Livia Fritz, the study's lead author. "We also saw that changes made at the individual level can lead to broader societal change provided they're supported by political action at the same time."[22]

> "It seems that the climate protests have effectively raised awareness and influenced the public discourse on climate issues."[21]
>
> —Ishan Bipin Ajmera, a postdoctoral researcher at the University of Natural Resources and Life Sciences

Impacting Policies

Student protests can impact policies in schools, communities, and governments. Students have been highly involved in protests calling for equality and social justice for decades. In May 2020 the murder of George Floyd, a Black man, at the hands of Minneapolis police officers brought the issues of police brutality and racial justice once again into the spotlight. Protesters marched and rallied in cities worldwide, including Paris, London, and New York. Students took the lead in protests on many college and high school campuses.

Within days of Floyd's murder, students planned Black Lives Matter (BLM) marches nationwide. The BLM movement originated in 2013 after the acquittal of the man who fatally shot Black teen Trayvon Martin. Since its founding, BLM has worked for racial justice and equality, and student activists have taken a significant role in BLM's protest activity. In June 2020 high school students from Katy Independent School District in Katy, Texas, organized a protest to honor Floyd and speak out against police brutality. Word of the event spread quickly on social media, and more than one thousand protesters attended the march and listened to a series of speakers. Seventeen-year-old Erika Alverez was one of the student organizers. "It's a way to speak out about systemic racism in America, to organize Katy under that common goal, and to recognize the issues prevalent in our society,"[23] Alverez says.

In addition to protesting police violence, students are leading efforts on campus to get their schools to increase diversity on campus, cut ties with police, and create equal educational opportunities for all students, no matter whether they are wealthy or poor. In many cases their efforts have led to change on campus. For example, at the University of Iowa, faculty in the College of Liberal Arts and Sciences (CLAS) established a virtual series in 2021 that highlights racial justice issues in many areas, including housing, media, health, and policing. The series provides discussions and performances that university faculty can use in their classrooms. "The values of diversity, equity, and inclusion are at the heart of the liberal arts and sciences, and CLAS is committed to realizing them in its classrooms, labs, and studios,"[24] says Sara

Anti-apartheid Protests in the 1980s

In the 1980s students on US college campuses protested apartheid, a system of racial segregation in South Africa that had existed since the late 1940s. After increasingly repressive actions by the South African government, the US student movement gained momentum in 1985 and grew into a massive protest movement. Some of the first student-led demonstrations occurred at Columbia University in New York City. After students at Cornell University in Ithaca, New York, put up a tent encampment, similar tent communities spread nationwide. Before long, students at nearly fifty universities were protesting in such encampments. At more than 150 universities, students held protests and demonstrations. They called for the United States to boycott South African products, divest from investments in South Africa, and impose sanctions on the country. As students and other activists kept up the pressure, the protests had an impact. Many universities began to divest from South Africa, and some banks began to pull their loans from the country. Also, in 1986 Congress passed the 1986 Comprehensive Anti-Apartheid Act, which imposed sanctions against South Africa and aimed to help end apartheid.

Sanders, the CLAS interim dean and director of diversity, equity, and inclusion (DEI).

Other changes being made at the University of Iowa include reevaluating hiring processes to recruit more diverse candidates, requiring each department to develop an antiracist action plan, and creating a DEI program to support faculty with their research and work focused on race, racism, and racial gaps. A student-led DEI advisory committee will also identify barriers impacting student success. "Our success depends on the diversity of our students, faculty, and staff by creating an environment where all can thrive," says Liz Tovar, University of Iowa's interim associate vice president for DEI. "Continuing to improve the campus climate requires sustained, community-wide effort, which is critical to the future success of the university."[25]

Student-led protests can have a powerful impact for the causes that youths support. When students join together in marches, demonstrations, sit-ins, and other protest activities, they can increase awareness about their causes. In many cases, students have gotten results and inspired change in their local communities and the larger worldwide community.

CHAPTER THREE

Protest Pitfalls and Backlash

Student protests can be a powerful way to highlight important issues, bring about policy changes, and drive social change. However, student protests can have unintended consequences, negatively impacting students, campus communities, and the public.

Balancing the Rights of Many

When students participate in rallies, sit-ins, marches, and other protest activities, they exercise some of the most fundamental American rights: to express themselves freely and to peacefully assemble. However, although the First Amendment protects the right of students to protest at universities, some forms of protest can violate the rights of others. "There's a point when you cross over from free speech into activity that can be precluded. That's blocking access to buildings, that's occupying buildings, that's disrupting the orderly operation of the institution, as well as actually engaging in threatening behavior, violent behavior,"[26] says Frederick Lawrence, lawyer and civil rights scholar.

The conflict between the rights of protesters and the rights of other students was highlighted during the protests regarding the Israel-Hamas War on university campuses during the spring of 2024. At the University of California, Santa Cruz, pro-Palestinian student protesters set up a protest encampment on the campus's Quarry Plaza in early May, with students calling for the university to divest from institutions affiliated with Israel. Several days later, protesters moved the encampment from the plaza to the campus's main entrance. They blocked the roadway with wood, shipping pallets, rocks, and other debris. Protesters stood in the roadway blocking the campus entrance, chanting and calling for the end of Israel's occupation of Palestine. Faculty, staff, and students on campus could not leave, while others arriving for class or work could not enter the university's campus.

On May 28 university chancellor Cynthia Larive issued a statement condemning the protest activities that infringed on the rights of others on campus and created a dangerous situation. "Blocking entrances is unlawful and infringes on the rights of our students, faculty, and staff, who are trying to learn, teach, and go about their lives," she stated. "As a community, we rely on one another to promote the safety and inclusion of others. The actions taken today harmed our entire campus community."[27]

> "There's a point when you cross over from free speech into activity that can be precluded. That's blocking access to buildings, that's occupying buildings, that's disrupting the orderly operation of the institution, as well as actually engaging in threatening behavior, violent behavior."[26]
>
> —Frederick Lawrence, lawyer and civil rights scholar

Disrupting Campus Operations

In some cases student protest activities can disrupt campus operations and cause changes to or even the cancellation of classes for other students. In the spring of 2024, several universities shut down in-person classes or switched to remote learning as protest demonstrations grew on campus, including Barnard College, California State Polytechnic University, City College of New York, Columbia University, Tulane University, and the University of California, Los Angeles. Even classes that remained in-person experienced some disruption. At Barnard College in New York City, students were forced to take end-of-semester final exams remotely after in-person classes were canceled. Amy Gallatin, the mother of a Barnard freshman, described her daughter's finals experience as challenging: "My daughter is also frustrated [and] understandably so. She had a final exam yesterday at 6 o'clock that she was taking from her dorm only to have the protesters on the street banging and clanging and chanting."[28]

Disruptive student protests in support of Gaza led some universities, including Tulane University in Louisiana (pictured), to shift some in-person classes to remote learning.

For some universities, campus disruptions led to the cancellation of graduation ceremonies. For example, Columbia University and the University of Southern California canceled their main graduation ceremonies, while other schools, such as Emory University, moved graduation ceremonies to different locations. For the class of 2024, the cancellation of graduation ceremonies hit hard, since most of these seniors also had their high school graduations canceled in 2020 due to the COVID-19 pandemic.

However, some people argue that disruption of regular activity is the most effective way to get people's attention, one of the main goals of protest. "Part of the logic of protest is to try and disrupt the status quo, is to say some kind of inequality or injustice is no longer acceptable," says Omar Wasow, assistant professor of political science at the University of California, Berkeley. "[This] disruption is meant to say we no longer accept what is the current norm, but that means potentially inconveniencing or doing things that make people in positions of power or people who are more established uncomfortable,"[29]

Threats and Harassment

Student protests can also cross the line when other students and campus community members feel threatened, particularly when they are harassed or face discrimination. The intense emotions involved in the Israeli-Palestinian protests created an atmosphere on several campuses in which both Jewish and Muslim students felt uncomfortable. More than half of Jewish and Muslim students and nearly 20 percent of all college students reported feeling unsafe on campus because of their views on the Israeli-Palestinian conflict, according to a March 2024 report by the University of Chicago Project on Security and Threats.

At Columbia University, Jewish students reported being harassed or experiencing anti-Semitism from protesters. In a statement condemning hate speech, New York City mayor Eric Adams called out specific examples on Columbia's campus, in-

---

Silencing Opposing Viewpoints

In some cases student protests have silenced people with differing opinions. For example, in 2023 protesters at the State University of New York at Albany shut down conservative speaker Ian Haworth, who had been invited to campus to discuss free speech. Protesters, who accused Haworth of being transphobic, filled the campus meeting room and chanted epithets. They formed a conga line and danced around the room. When a conservative student attempted to speak, protesters shouted over him. Also, in 2023 a group of student protesters shouted down a federal appellate judge's speech at Stanford Law School. Dozens of student protesters attended the campus event, enraged that Judge Kyle Duncan had refused to use an offender's preferred pronouns in a case opinion. The protesters heckled Duncan so he could not give his prepared speech. Nico Perrino from the Foundation for Individual Rights and Expression explains that these students do not understand free speech rights. "Shouting down speakers is just like any other form of censorship: It's the few deciding for the many what they can hear. Protesters have every right to engage in peaceful, nondisruptive protest. But they do not have the right to take over someone else's event and make it their own," he says.

Nico Perrino, "College Campus Hecklers, Your Disruptions Don't Count as Free Speech," *Los Angeles Times*, April 14, 2023. www.latimes.com.

In October 2023, Jewish students at Columbia University speak about threats, harassment, and violence on campus. They say the university has failed to protect them from antisemitic acts stemming from protests in support of Gaza.

cluding "a young woman holding a sign with an arrow pointing to Jewish students stating 'Al-Qasam's Next Targets'." Adams recognized the protester's cause but reminded them that their right to protest did not give them the right to harass or persecute others. "I know the conflict in the Middle East has left many of us grieving and angry. New Yorkers have every right to express their sorrow, but that heartbreak does not give anyone the right to harass or threaten others or to physically harm someone they disagree with."[30]

School Responsibilities and Responses

Historically, college and university campuses have fiercely supported students' right to free expression and committed to being a place for students to assemble and protest the issues that move them. However, schools are also responsible for ensuring the safety of all campus community members and fostering an environment in which hate is not accepted. When protests occur, schools must find a way to balance the rights and safety of the entire campus community.

In the face of student protests, schools have chosen different ways to strike that balance. During the 2024 antiwar demonstrations, some universities—such as Northwestern, Brown, and Johns Hopkins—chose to negotiate with student protesters and come to an agreement that both sides could accept. For example, at Northwestern, administrators agreed with students on how to take down their protest encampment. "We thought the best way to sustainably de-escalate the situation was to actually talk with our students. We have a good sustainable agreement which provides a number of things that the students wanted and that we wanted to do,"[31] says Northwestern president Michael Schill. Northwestern's agreement allowed students to hold peaceful demonstrations without tents throughout the spring semester. At the same time, the university committed to adding student representation on the school's investment committee, bringing more Palestinian students to campus, and more. Other schools have agreed to provide more transparency on their endowments, provide scholarships or aid for Palestinian students, and limit disciplinary action for student protesters.

In other cases universities have stood firm on enforcing campus rules. On some campuses, university officials have called local police to clear protest encampments and arrest students for trespassing, vandalism, and other charges. For example, at the University of Pennsylvania, university officials called in local police after negotiations with student protesters failed to lead to an agreement. On May 10, 2024, campus police and Philadelphia police officers arrived at dawn dressed in riot gear to clear out the student protest encampment. "Protestors were given multiple warnings that they were trespassing and offered the opportunity to voluntarily leave and avoid citation," says a spokesperson for the university. "Those who chose to stay did so knowing that they would be arrested

> "We thought the best way to sustainably de-escalate the situation was to actually talk with our students. We have a good sustainable agreement which provides a number of things that the students wanted and that we wanted to do."[31]
>
> —Michael Schill, president of Northwestern University

and removed."[32] Thirty-three individuals were arrested, including at least nine students.

The use of police to break up student protests has sparked fierce debate. For some, police action is necessary to restore order, ensure safety, and protect the school's core operations. They also point out that police action and potential arrest are consequences of breaking university rules and codes of conduct. For others, however, bringing police on campus violates trust between students and university administrators. Robert Cohen, a history professor at New York University, says:

> Police helmets and zip ties are never going to convince students to moderate their rhetoric and build a more inclusive antiwar movement. Such rethinking can only come from dialogue, trust, and community building, all of which are short-circuited by college presidents, donors, and politicians when they treat some of their campus' most idealistic, politically engaged students—who on my campus slept outside in the rain to protest the Gaza war—as if they were criminals.[33]

Police detain a protester on the University of Pennsylvania campus in May 2024. Some university officials have called police to clear protest encampments and arrest students for trespassing, vandalism, and other charges.

Potential Consequences

While the First Amendment protects free speech and the right to gather for peaceful protest, it does not shield student protesters from potential consequences from protest activities. Public and private universities are allowed to place some reasonable restrictions on the time, place, and manner of public assemblies. When attending a university, students agree to follow the school's campus rules and regulations. When protest activities break campus rules, students can face various disciplinary actions. Some have been arrested and now have a criminal record, while others have been suspended or expelled.

For University of Chicago student Youssef Hasweh, the decision to participate in pro-Palestinian campus protests has jeopardized his college degree. Hasweh is one of several students who had their degrees withheld by the university pending an investigation into their connection to a campus protest encampment. "Four years and just a criminal record, nothing else. A decade of (high school and college) work down the toilet because I decided to express my free speech,"[34] says Hasweh. In a worst-case scenario, expelled students often still owe the student debt they incurred to attend college. Without a degree, finding a job in their chosen field will likely be more difficult and may require them to change plans.

The Effectiveness of Protests Varies

Millions of students have joined campus protests for various causes nationwide. However, many question whether protests are an effective way to drive meaningful change. The evidence is mixed, according to researchers who study protest movements. Sometimes, protests can influence media coverage, public opinion, and policies in the short term. For example, research suggests that the 1960s civil rights protests and the 2020 BLM protests affected how people voted and thereby impacted elections. Longer-term changes in public opinion and policies can be more challenging to link to protests directly.

Researchers say several factors can impact a protest movement's success or failure. Large protests are generally more effective than smaller ones, while nonviolent protests are often more impactful than violent ones. Another factor is having clear, unified goals. Demonstrators are more likely to successfully drive change if their demands are clear and unified, instead of wide-ranging and unconnected. "When power holders are hearing a hodgepodge of demands, they struggle to interpret what the group wants,"[35] says Lisa Mueller, a researcher studying social movements at Macalester College in Saint Paul, Minnesota.

Repression by law enforcement can gain sympathy for protesters, according to researchers. Some studies have shown that violent repression of civil rights protests led to media coverage that was sympathetic to the protesters and their cause. In contrast, violent protests were reported in the media as riots. "Non-violence is effective. But what's especially effective is non-violence met by repression," says Omar Wasow. Wasow points to the 2024 student protests at Columbia University as an example. When university officials called police to clear students, most of whom were engaged in nonviolent protest, it increased media attention and sparked student protests nationwide. "It crystallized national attention and gave them a common tactic,"[36] Wasow says.

Public Opinion Matters

For a protest to be effective, demonstrators must get public opinion on their side. Public opinion has an important role in guiding individual behavior. For example, if a person's friends start taking public transportation and biking to reduce fossil fuel use, that individual is more likely to also increase use of public transportation and other low-emission modes of transportation. Also, widespread public opinion can influence government policy changes by as much as 75 percent. According to policy makers, legislators often look at large protest movements and media coverage of these events to understand where the public falls on a given issue. The more people involved in a protest, the more of an impact it can have. Also, polls suggests that when a cause is already popular, disruptive protests do not always threaten public support for it.

Researchers like Mueller are attempting to use their work to help activists and protest movements. "Social protest and larger-scale social action is a way to generate social change—but that doesn't mean it always will. And we're still trying to figure out when it will and when it won't,"[37] says Eric Shuman, a social psychologist at New York University.

> "No matter the frustration of campus activists or their desire to be heard, true civil disobedience shouldn't violate the rights of others."[38]
>
> —David French, *New York Times* columnist

Student voices in protest can have a powerful impact, bringing attention to important causes and inspiring needed change. But in some cases protests cross the line from free expression to violating the rights of others. David French, a *New York Times* columnist, says,

> What we're seeing on a number of campuses isn't free expression, nor is it civil disobedience. It's outright lawlessness. No matter the frustration of campus activists or their desire to be heard, true civil disobedience shouldn't violate the rights of others. Indefinitely occupying a quad violates the rights of other speakers to use the same space. Relentless, loud protest violates the rights of students to sleep or study in peace. And when protests become truly threatening or intimidating, they can violate the civil rights of other students, especially if those students are targeted on the basis of their race, sex, color or national origin.[38]

When this happens, protests can become less effective for the causes they promote.

CHAPTER FOUR

Vandalism and Violence on Campus

Few students expect protests to become violent. Most protests begin peacefully and remain peaceful. However, when emotions run high and confrontations occur, protests can sometimes escalate into violence and vandalism. While violent actions can grab the public's attention and make media headlines, they can also put people and property at risk and carry legal consequences.

Clashes Between Protesters

People who disagree with student protesters may organize a counterprotest on campus. Just as student protesters have the right to express their views and assemble, those who disagree with them have the right to express their dissent in a counterprotest or similar demonstration. Often, counterprotesters will organize near the protesters with whom they disagree. However, tensions can rise quickly between the groups. If left unchecked, the tension can spill into violence.

In late April 2024 protesters and counterprotesters clashed at the University of California, Los Angeles (UCLA). Earlier that month, pro-Palestinian protesters set up dozens of tents in an encampment on Dickson Plaza, a central green space on the UCLA campus. Tensions rose when counterprotesters from the school's Israeli-American Council, an advocacy group, held a large rally near the encampment. The dueling rallies were large and noisy but mainly remained peaceful. UCLA officials used metal barriers to separate the two protest groups and establish a physical buffer zone between them. These efforts appeared to work for a time, and no major conflicts were reported.

On April 30, a crowd of pro-Israel counterprotesters gathered near the pro-Palestinian encampment. That evening, counterprotesters attempted to forcefully remove the barriers around the tent encampment. As fights broke out between some of the protesters and counterprotesters, some people set off fireworks or sprayed pepper spray and other irritants. Others threw chairs, plywood, and other objects. The chaos continued for several hours until police were able to get the campus under control. "Horrific acts of violence occurred at the encampment tonight. . . . We are sickened by this senseless violence and it must end,"[39] said Mary Osako, a UCLA vice chancellor.

A clash between pro-Palestinian demonstrators and pro-Israel demonstrators took place in April 2024 at UCLA (pictured). University officials had erected a barrier between the two groups to prevent conflict.

Shock Value

Sometimes, student protesters use violence and vandalism to shock the public and draw attention to their cause. In 2020 students at Northwestern University in Evanston, Illinois, called on university officials to cut ties with local and campus police departments as part of a larger nationwide protest movement against police brutality. In early June, students presented university officials with a petition with more than eight thousand signatures, urging the university to disband its campus police and redirect funding to causes supporting Black students' well-being. Northwestern committed to reviewing campus police operations but stopped short of disbanding the unit.

Unsatisfied, students started daily protest marches in October 2020. On October 17 some students turned to vandalism to get their message across. They spray-painted abolitionist and anti-capitalist messages on Evanston sidewalks and buildings. At least one protester smashed a storefront window. Protesters also burned a school banner, vandalized campus property, and lit fires. In response, Northwestern president Morton Schapiro released a statement: "To those protesters and their supporters who justify such actions, I ask you to take a long hard look in the mirror and realize that this isn't actually 'speaking truth to power' or furthering your cause. It is an abomination and you should be ashamed of yourselves,"[40] he wrote.

However, LaTesha Harris, a recent Northwestern graduate involved in the protests, blames Schapiro and Northwestern officials who ignored the students' concerns for months. "It's really disheartening to see that Northwestern only is responding to our campaign now because we're acting 'destructive,'"[41] said Harris. For months, the students held marches, protests, sit-ins, and other peaceful events that did not damage property. However, their efforts were largely ignored by the university. According to Harris, these feelings led some students to express themselves

> "To those protesters and their supporters who justify such actions, I ask you to take a long hard look in the mirror and realize that this isn't actually 'speaking truth to power' or furthering your cause."[40]
>
> —Morton Schapiro, president of Northwestern University

Clashes at Emory

At Emory University in Atlanta, Georgia, police responded quickly when called to remove protest encampments in April 2024. Dozens of armed Atlanta police officers and Georgia state troopers arrived on campus and used pepper balls, stun guns, and rubber bullets to clear protesting students, faculty, and community members. Police arrested at least twenty-eight people after university president Gregory Fenves called them to the school. Emory professor Emil' Keme saw the violence firsthand when he arrived on campus for class. As Keme walked over to the crowd of student protesters, police began moving the crowd. "Police immediately began to force people to move. I felt like I was in a war zone, with all the police and their weapons, the rubber bullets. We were pushed away. I held on to one of my students. Police took the student next to me, pushed an older lady nearby and then pushed me," he says. Keme was arrested and charged with disorderly conduct, a misdemeanor. Keme says the violent experience was traumatic. "The university is supposed to be a place of ideas, of dialogue and freedom of speech. All of that came crumbling down," he says.

Quoted in Timothy Pratt, "'Like a War Zone': Emory University Grapples with Fallout from Police Response to Protest," *The Guardian* (Manchester, UK), April 27, 2024. www.theguardian.com.

spontaneously through graffiti and vandalism. "People who show up to our actions—if they're feeling frustrated and they're feeling angry and they decide that the way they want to take it out is by doing vandalism or graffiti or burning something, that's up to them. We're not here to police anyone. We're here to honestly cause a disruption and get on Northwestern University's radar, and it's frustrating that the only way to do that, as we've seen, is for these 'violent' things to happen,"[42] said Harris.

Police Response Matters

When school officials call law enforcement to campus, how police officers react to protesters often has a significant effect on whether a protest remains peaceful or escalates into violence. When the police have a strong relationship with students and the local community, and both sides are willing to work together, campus protests are more likely to remain peaceful. However, tensions can quickly rise when even a few people confront officers. "Riots are a product of interactions—largely to do with the nature of the way police treats crowds," explains Professor Clifford Stott, an expert in crowd behavior at Keele University in England. Stott explains that when police officers face confrontation, their reaction is often directed toward the entire crowd. When this occurs, some people feel that the police reaction is unjustified, which strengthens an "us versus them" viewpoint. According to Stott, this "can change the way people feel about violence and confrontation—for example, they may start feeling that violence is legitimate given the circumstances."[43] For example, when police use rubber bullets, tear gas, pepper spray, and other methods to control protest crowds, these tactics can worsen tensions and lead to more violence.

At Kent State University in Ohio, the infamous armed response to protesters in 1970 plunged the campus into violence and resulted in the deaths of four students. At the time, anti–Vietnam War protests were common on college campuses nationwide. When President Richard Nixon announced the invasion of Cambodia by US forces, new protests broke out at Kent State. After a violent confrontation between local police and protesters, some Kent storefronts were vandalized. Clashes between police and

In 1970 members of the National Guard opened fire on Kent State University students who were protesting the Vietnam War. Four students died.

protesters continued for two days. At one point, a Reserve Officer Training Corps building on the Kent State campus was burned down. On May 4 student organizers called for another antiwar protest on campus. By then the Ohio National Guard had arrived to protect the campus and town at the request of the Kent mayor. University officials had banned further campus demonstrations, but many students either did not know or did not care. By late morning, about three thousand people had gathered on campus. A chaotic confrontation erupted when the National Guard attempted to disperse the crowd. Guardsmen used tear gas on students and fired live ammunition into the crowd.

Roseann Canfora was one of the Kent State students protesting that day. "My brother's roommate pulled me behind a parked car, and it was at that moment that I realized this was live ammunition because the car was riddled with bullets. The glass of the car windows was shattering above us, and we could hear the M1 bullets zipping past our heads and bumping into the ground in the pavement around us. And it was a horrifying 13 seconds,"[44] she says. Four students died, and nine others were wounded, including Canfora's brother, Alan.

The violent shootings shocked the nation and triggered protests on college campuses nationwide. The Kent State shootings also had a significant effect on public opinion, turning many against the Vietnam War. Years later, the Kent State tragedy remains a reminder of what can happen when protests turn violent.

Impact on Public Opinion

From the Greensboro sit-ins to international climate strikes, peaceful protests have had a powerful and lasting impact. They have inspired movements that have shaped the world to be a better place. However, some worry that when protests turn violent, it can alienate people who might support the cause. Gordana Rabrenovic, associate professor of sociology at Northeastern University, explains that peace and consensus are essential for a movement to gather support and inspire lasting change. "There's

> "There's certainly more evidence that peaceful protests are more successful because they build a wider coalition. Violence can scare away your potential allies."[45]
>
> —Gordana Rabrenovic, associate professor of sociology at Northeastern University

certainly more evidence that peaceful protests are more successful because they build a wider coalition," she says. "Violence can scare away your potential allies. You need the people on the sidelines to say, 'This is my issue, too.'"[45]

Research from Stanford University supports the view that violence can reduce support for protesters and their causes. According to studies by Stanford sociologist Robb Willer, when protesters use violence, people can see them as unreasonable, which can lead to fewer people identifying with the group and its cause. And in some cases the use of violence can even increase support for the other side. Willer says:

> Violence cannot always be avoided, such as when it is used in self-defense. But our results do fit well with other work suggesting that violent activism typically turns people off, including potential supporters, and that it builds opposition to those who use it. If people understood clearly the effects of violent protest on public opinion, they might try harder to convince other activists on their side not to use these tactics.[46]

However, others argue that in some situations, violence is necessary and even more effective. "The reality is that—objectively examining protests—violent protest has a positive impact on political and policy change. Nonviolent protest brings awareness to an issue; violent protest brings urgency to an issue,"[47] says Daniel Gillion, a University of Pennsylvania professor and expert on civil rights protests. For example, the Kent State shootings triggered a nationwide student

> "The reality is that—objectively examining protests—violent protest has a positive impact on political and policy change. Nonviolent protest brings awareness to an issue; violent protest brings urgency to an issue."[47]
>
> —Daniel Gillion, professor at the University of Pennsylvania

strike in which millions of students protested and forced the closure of many universities and colleges. Newspapers and magazines published stories and photographs from the massacre, including an iconic photo of a young woman screaming as she knelt by the body of a dead student. The violent shootings are credited with turning the public against the Vietnam War. Some historians have also argued that the Kent State violence was one factor in the failure of President Nixon's administration.

Preventing Violent Protests

Schools have taken different approaches to preventing protests from becoming violent on campus. Some schools, like Brown University, have negotiated with student protesters. After a weeklong protest in a tent encampment on the school campus in 2024, Brown students agreed to take down their tents in exchange for a seat at the upcoming meeting with the Corporation of Brown University. "Universities were built to hold disagreement and grapple with competing views. This is an essential part of our mission of

Standoff at Stanford

In June 2024 thirteen Stanford students and alumni barricaded themselves in the university president's office to protest against the Israel-Hamas War. The protesters refused to leave the office until school administrators and the board of trustees agreed to account for their role in profiting from ongoing war in Gaza. The protesters accused the university of holding millions of dollars in investments in companies that provided support and supplies to Israel's military. According to Stanford officials, the protesters shoved and injured a public safety officer, were responsible for significant damage to the building's interior, and committed extensive vandalism to several campus buildings. The school called police, who arrested the protesters and removed them from campus. Adam Swart, founder of Crowds on Demand, specializes in organizing advocacy events and believes the tactics used by the Stanford protesters were not smart. "You're making it very easy to reduce the entire movement, the entire pro Palestine movement into the most violent, absurd, misguided acts, instead of keeping the focus on your core talking points about the human rights matter at hand," says Swart.

Quoted in Gloria Rodriquez and Zach Fuentes, "Stanford Students Arrested for Barricading in President's Office, Allegedly Leaving 'Vile' Graffiti," ABC 7 News, June 5, 2024. https://abc7news.com.

Rain batters a pro-Palestinian encampment at the University of Pennsylvania in May 2024. The university later temporarily banned on-campus encampments and overnight demonstrations to prevent violence and vandalism.

advancing knowledge and understanding,"[48] Brown's president, Christina Paxson, wrote in a letter announcing the agreement.

Some schools have implemented new rules to prevent protest activity from escalating into violence and vandalism. For example, the University of Pennsylvania temporarily banned encampments and overnight demonstrations on campus in 2024. The new rules, which are the first that specifically ban encampments, will be reviewed by a faculty-led committee during the 2024–2025 school year. Violators will be considered trespassers and will face consequences. The university made the rule changes after antiwar protesters set up tents on campus for more than two weeks during the spring of 2024, which had to be removed by campus and city police. The new guidelines aim to establish where, when, and how student expression can occur on campus. Schools hope to avoid clashes with protesters that could turn violent by establishing clear guidelines.

Even with clear guidelines, schools often disagree on what amount of disruption calls for police action. At some schools, administrators believe law enforcement should be called when school rules are violated. For example, at Dartmouth College, officials called police to clear protesters only two hours after the protesters had set up tents, violating campus rules. At Harvard University, however, the trigger for police involvement is higher. Harvard officials will not call Boston police unless there is significant property damage or any physical violence.

When emotions run high during protests on campus, peaceful actions can escalate into violent acts. While violence can attract media attention and make headlines, it also risks turning public opinion against a cause. In some cases, protest violence may even increase support for the opposing side. Jack Radey, who protested as a student in the 1960s, reminds students to be smart about protests. "In general, threatening violence, or doing it, whether by destroying property, or disrupting a speaker or class, or throwing rocks at police who are not violently trying to prevent people from exercising their constitutional rights, is counterproductive, stupid,"[49] says Radey.

CHAPTER FIVE

Future of Student Protests

In recent years more people have gathered in protest in countries worldwide. Protesters have taken a stand against war, injustice, climate change, inequality, political authorities, and other issues. According to one global study, annual protests more than tripled from 2006 to 2020. "That increase in activism has eclipsed even the turbulent 1960s. We really are in an empirically exceptional time of global protests,"[50] says Lisa Mueller, a social and political scientist at Macalester College in Saint Paul, Minnesota.

Students on the Front Lines

As protests become more common, students and young people are increasingly on the front lines. According to a 2024 UNICEF report on youths and protests, today's young people generally prefer informal political activities such as protests, petitions, or boycotts over more formal actions such as being a member of a political party or voting. "Some believe this is because young people have greater interest in issue-based politics and action that requires no intermediaries, rather than in traditional, institutionalized politics,"[51] write the report's authors.

The UNICEF report also found that young people are more likely to protest than older people. This finding may be due to a combination of factors, including their preference for direct action based on ideological viewpoints. Many of today's college students were in middle and high school during the Black Lives Matter protests and view protests as a regular part of civic engagement. Omar Wasow, assistant professor of political science at the University of California, Berkeley, says,

> Protest movements definitely ebb and flow across generations. And so there was a peak in protest activity in the '60s and then a bit of a lull. And then we've seen . . . during wars, or in the case of the 2020 Black Lives Matter movement, a resurgence. And so I think there are some generations that are more defined by protest movements than others. Importantly, also, the Black Lives Matter protests of 2020 were among the biggest protest movements in American history. And so that really was a defining experience for people coming of age in that period.[52]

Today's youths experienced the Great Recession of 2008 and witnessed social unrest and division. Their lives have also been upended by the COVID-19 pandemic, increasing global inequalities, and the threat of climate change. "The sense of crisis right now is amplified," says Jessica Taft, an associate professor of

Young people take part in a Black Lives Matter protest in California in 2020. Many of today's college students, who were in secondary school around this time, view protests as a regular part of civic engagement.

> "The sense of crisis right now is amplified. The extent of the climate crisis, the profound inequalities, the global creep of fascism—they are all existential threats."[53]
>
> —Jessica Taft, associate professor of Latin American and Latino studies at the University of California, Santa Cruz

Latin American and Latino studies at the University of California, Santa Cruz. "The extent of the climate crisis, the profound inequalities, the global creep of fascism—they are all existential threats."[53] According to Taft, these historical moments have shaped how young people see the world and influenced the role of activism in their lives. For example, many youths see climate change as threatening earth's survival and have become increasingly vocal in climate movements and demands for change. Subir Sinha, a lecturer in development studies at the University of London, says,

> The idea that there may not be a future, or if there is one, it could be heavily diminished, plays heavy on their minds. Climate-change activism used to deal with abstract scientific concepts, but with annual forest fires, floods, drought and record heat, plus the news and social-media coverage of all this, we can feel climate [change] accelerating, and that adds to a sense of impending apocalypse.[54]

Twenty-Four Hour Online News

Adding to the youths' sense of urgency about issues is how they are exposed to news and information. Unlike previous generations, today's young people can access news and other content around the clock from a smartphone in their palm. It does not matter where they are or what time it is; news websites, social media sites, search engines, and streaming channels always provide information. Additionally, with social media sites, the news has become participatory. Anyone can comment, share, like, and add content on social media.

With news becoming more accessible, youths are consuming more news, according to a 2022 digital media trends survey by Deloitte. Nearly 80 percent of teens aged fourteen to nineteen get news daily from at least one source, and they prefer getting their news on social sites and digital news sources. About half of the teens reported they got news daily from their social media feeds or messaging apps, while 40 percent got news from search engines. The teens preferred these news sources because they were more immediate, interactive, and engaging than traditional television news or newspaper articles. Teens can follow and connect with like-minded content creators on social media sites. These platforms and their creators have become centers for news and information for millions of followers worldwide.

The Deloitte survey also found that mobile devices like smartphones are essential for providing news and information to teens. Nearly two-thirds of teens who follow news and current events reported getting most of their information from alerts or other notifications on their mobile devices. More than half said they consumed news only on their smartphones. With mobile devices providing around-the-clock access to news and information, it can be difficult for teens and others to escape. The constant press of information can raise the urgency teens feel about the issues that are important to them, driving them to act.

Most teens who follow news and current events get that information on their smartphones and other mobile devices. Having around-the-clock access can heighten the sense of urgency about issues.

Going Global Online

As more youths step forward to act on the issues they support, they are bringing protest activities into the spaces where they have grown up: digital spaces. While previous generations have leaned on grassroots activism and in-person demonstrations, today's youths are speaking out about many of the same issues—climate crisis, LGBTQ+ rights, gun control, racial justice, and gender equality—online. There, they can express their political views and identities creatively, from noting preferred pronouns and sexual orientation in an Instagram bio or joining like-minded groups on the chat room platform Discord. They feel comfortable online, and nearly half say that the internet makes them feel their voices matter, according to a 2020 study from the UK Safer Internet Centre.

In the digital world, youths have seemingly endless ways to find inspiration, spread information, and mobilize groups of like-minded people. While previous generations passed out leaflets, made phone calls, and knocked on neighborhood doors to generate support for a movement, today's youths communicate and collaborate with others online. Teen activists create TikTok videos, podcasts, and other content for their causes. They circulate online petitions and use hashtags to link individual social media posts and create collective action. They share news on the ground as it happens. For example, young people who were part of the Black Lives Matter movement posted videos and other content online to document injustices and call for accountability, which shined a bright spotlight on their cause. "There are newer mechanisms through which they are mobilizing collectively,"[55] says Subir Sinha.

The use of digital technology significantly differs in youth political activity compared to older generations, according to Sinha. "They understand certain mediums so much better, and know how to make things go viral in a way, unlike those of us who weren't born into computer and mobile phone culture."[56] The internet and smartphones have given youths louder and wider-reaching voices as activists. Elijah McKenzie-Jackson, a teen activist passionate about climate issues, agrees that the internet and social media give teens a powerful tool for protest. "This allows us to narrate our own stories, which is why I think Gen Z has succeeded in so many activism efforts. We are wholly interlinked to connect across the world,"[57] he says.

Social media sites have proved to be an effective and lower-cost platform to gather support, share information, and organize protests. People worldwide have recognized the power of social media to bring awareness to issues. A 2022 Pew Research Center survey of nineteen advanced economies found that a median of 77 percent of respondents believed that social media effectively increases public awareness about social and political issues. Most people surveyed (65 percent median) also believed that social media was effective at changing other people's viewpoints on social and political issues. Slightly fewer respondents believed that social media was an effective way to influence their government's policy decisions (61 percent median).

Social media's global reach has given today's young people the ability to raise awareness about the issues they care about to a worldwide audience. As a result, social movements are increasingly going global. Youth-led movements such as Black Lives Matter, School Strike for Climate, and March for Our Lives have gained followers and momentum online, which has led to in-person protest events and rallies in countries worldwide. Young protesters document local events on social media, encouraging others to join and

Raising Funds

The internet is an efficient platform for raising funds for a cause. Crowdfunding sites like GoFundMe, Kickstarter, and Indiegogo allow people to raise money online from individual donors. These campaigns are quick and easy to set up, and organizers can quickly access any money raised. Organizers can set up crowdfunding campaigns for various events, such as protest marches or talks from noted speakers. Often, campaign organizers use social media posts or crowdfunding websites to ask for donations. Each crowdfunding platform has a set of rules on how to set up a campaign, what fees it will charge, and how it will release raised funds to the campaign organizer. Since the money raised goes directly to the campaign organizer, the organizer must be trustworthy and honest about the cause and how the funds will be used.

Online Protests

Some students have taken protests to online spaces. Protesters can participate in virtual sit-ins, a type of electronic civil disobedience. To conduct a virtual sit-in, protesters organize simultaneous and repeated web traffic to a chosen website. The increase in traffic disrupts the website's performance and can even cause it to crash. In February 2022 Generation Z activists targeted coffee chain Starbucks with an online protest after the company fired workers who had been attempting to establish a union. The youth activists launched a campaign called Change Is Brewing to flood Starbucks websites with fake online job applications. They created computer code allowing protesters to submit fake applications every twenty seconds automatically. Within the first week, more than ten thousand fake applications were sent. Campaign leader Elise Joshi, an operations director with the activist group Gen-Z for Change, posted a video on X (formerly Twitter) that called for people to join the online protest. "This is just the beginning of Starbucks' anti-union efforts, and therefore just the beginning of our work with Change Is Brewing," says Joshi.

Quoted in Khaleda Rahman, "Gen-Z Activists Flood Starbucks with Fake Job Applications over Firings," *Newsweek*, February 23, 2022. www.newsweek.com.

plan their local efforts. "Youth voice from elementary to mid-20s matters because we are exposed to these things on social media, we are more connected in digital ways, especially across the nation and the globe. We are able to build solidarity now more than ever,"[58] says twenty-two-year-old youth activist Victoria Acuna.

No Plans to Slow Down

Today's students have no plans to slow down their activism. Youth participation in protests is expected to grow, according to a 2024 UNICEF report. The report's authors write:

> Young people recognize the imminent threats to their future and expect this will contribute to a surge in youth participation in protests and activism. The young generation understands that relying solely on adults to save the world is unrealistic, so a proactive approach is needed. They will become more confident, critical and professional advocates and will strengthen their capacities across different issues.[59]

In Louisiana, high school students are showing they are ready to embrace activism. After state lawmakers introduced several bills to restrict LGBTQ+ rights in 2023, students began holding protests, walking out of classes, signing petitions, making phone calls, and testifying before government officials to speak out against the legislation. "The spirit of activism has grown over the past couple of years along with this feeling of 'We're not sure that the adults are taking care of us anymore,'"[60] says Rebecca Cavalier, an English teacher at Ben Franklin High School in New Orleans.

For many young people, activism is more than something to do; it has become part of their identity. Because it has become an integral part of how they see themselves, activism will be essential to their future. British teen Elijah McKenzie-Jackson

> "Youth voice from elementary to mid-20s matters because we are exposed to these things on social media, we are more connected in digital ways, especially across the nation and the globe. We are able to build solidarity now more than ever."[58]
>
> —Victoria Acuna, twenty-two-year-old youth activist

Two British teenagers, including Elijah McKenzie-Jackson (right), protest a proposed coal mine in 2020. McKenzie-Jackson views activism, especially on climate issues, as an integral part of his life.

> "It's more of a community and family versus a workplace, which is probably why so many of us are involved in movements. It's about getting impactful work done in a way that makes us feel fulfilled."[61]
>
> —Elijah McKenzie-Jackson, youth activist

is an example of activism becoming part of his identity. At age ten, McKenzie-Jackson learned about the impact of climate change and greenhouse gas emissions related to livestock and animal products. He decided to become a vegan. Quickly, McKenzie-Jackson realized that he needed to do more to impact the climate issues he cared about. At age fifteen, he joined Extinction Rebellion Youth, the youth wing of a global environmental movement. Since 2019 he has organized and participated in climate strikes with several organizations. Today McKenzie-Jackson does not see his activism as a job but as an integral part of his life. "It's more of a community and family versus a workplace, which is probably why so many of us are involved in movements. It's about getting impactful work done in a way that makes us feel fulfilled,"[61] he says.

SOURCE NOTES

Introduction: Protests at Columbia University

1. Quoted in Olivia Land, "Columbia Students Erect 60 Tents on Main Lawn to Demand University Divest from Israel as President Grilled on Antisemitism," *New York Post*, April 17, 2024. https://nypost.com.
2. Quoted in AP News, "Police Arrest Dozens of Pro-Palestinian Protesters at Columbia, Including Congresswoman's Daughter," April 18, 2024. https://apnews.com.
3. Quoted in Kiara Alfonseca, "As Columbia University Protests on Israel-Hamas War Come to a Head, What to Know," ABC News, April 30, 2024. https://abcnews.go.com.
4. Quoted in Luis Ferre-Sadurni et al., "Some Jewish Students Are Targeted as Protests Continue at Columbia," *New York Times*, April 21, 2024. www.nytimes.com.
5. Quoted in Deepti Hajela, "The American Paradox of Protest: Celebrated and Condemned, Welcomed and Muzzled," AP News, May 5, 2024. www.apnews.com.

Chapter One: The Importance of Public Protest

6. US Constitution, Amendment I, Constitution Center. https://constitutioncenter.org.
7. Geoffrey Stone and Eugene Volokh, "Freedom of Speech and the Press," National Constitution Center, 2024. https://constitutioncenter.org.
8. Kevin Greenberg, "Protesting on College Campuses: FAQs Answered," Freedom Forum, 2024. www.freedomforum.org.
9. Quoted in Sarah Wood, "College Campus Protests: What Students Should Know Before Taking Action," *U.S. News & World Report*, May 6, 2024. www.usnews.com.
10. Quoted in Martin Luther King, Jr. Research and Education Institute, "Sit-Ins." https://kinginstitute.stanford.edu.
11. Quoted in Martin Luther King, Jr. Research and Education Institute, "Sit-Ins."
12. Quoted in UC Berkeley, "Free Speech," 2024. www.berkeley.edu.
13. F. Willis Johnson, "Protest as a Democratic Function," The Fulcrum, April 25, 2024. https://thefulcrum.us.

Chapter Two: The Power of Student Protests

14. Quoted in Ken Leiser, "Protesters Stage Sit-In at St. Louis University," *Cape Cod Times* (Barnstable County, MA), October 13, 2014. www.capecodtimes.com.
15. Quoted in Fox 2 Now, "Week-Long Sit-In Demonstration Ends at Saint Louis University Campus," October 18, 2014. https://fox2now.com.
16. Quoted in Fox 2 Now, "Week-Long Sit-In Demonstration Ends at Saint Louis University Campus."
17. Cameron Kasky, "Parkland Student: My Generation Won't Stand for This," CNN, February 20, 2018. www.cnn.com.
18. Quoted in March for Our Lives, "Two Years After the Bipartisan Safer Communities Act, MFOL Celebrates Progress and Urges Congress to Act Again," June 25, 2024. https://marchforourlives.org.
19. Quoted in Jon Keller, "Are Pro-Palestinian Student Protests Helping or Hurting Their Cause?," CBS News, April 24, 2024. www.cbsnews.com.
20. Quoted in Liam Gould, "How Greta Thunberg's Climate Strikes Became a Global Movement in a Year," Reuters, August 19, 2019. hwww.reuters.com.
21. Quoted in Fintan Burke, "5 Years of Fridays for Future: Researchers Say Climate Strikes Bring Slow but Sure Change," Euronews, September 15, 2023. www.euronews.com.
22. Quoted in Angela Symons, "Fridays for Future: Greta's School Strikes Led a Third of Swiss Citizens to Change Their Habits," Euronews, September 10, 2023. www.euronews.com.
23. Quoted in Hannah Mackenzie, "Student-Organized March Draws More than 1,000 Protesters in Katy," Click2Houston.com, June 4, 2020. www.click2houston.com.
24. Quoted in Sarah Wood, "Institutions Make Curricular Changes in Response to Black Lives Matter Flashpoint," Diverse Education, February 19, 2021. www.diverseeducation.com.
25. Quoted in Wood, "Institutions Make Curricular Changes in Response to Black Lives Matter Flashpoint."

Chapter Three: Protest Pitfalls and Backlash

26. Quoted in Amna Nawaz et al., "How Colleges Decide When to Call In Police to Break Up Campus Protests," *PBS NewsHour*, May 1, 2024. www.pbs.org.
27. Quoted in University of California, Santa Cruz, "On Blocking Campus," May 28, 2024. https://news.ucsc.edu.
28. Quoted in Kyle Morris, "Parents, Students Livid as Colleges Move Classes Online amid Anti-Israel Violence: 'Very Unsettling,'" Fox News, May 1, 2024. www.foxnews.com.

29. Quoted in Marc Rivers et al., "Will the Generational Divide on Support for Israel Impact the Presidential Election?," NPR, June 13, 2024. www.npr.org.
30. Quoted in City of New York, "Mayor Adams' Statement on Ongoing Protests at Columbia University," April 21, 2024. www.nyc.gov.
31. Quoted in Rachel Treisman, "What We Can Learn from 4 Schools That Have Reached Agreements with Gaza Protesters," WGBH, May 8, 2024. www.wgbh.org.
32. Quoted in Elea Castiglione, "Police in Riot Gear Arrest 33 Protesters, Including Penn Students, at Gaza Solidarity Encampment," Daily Pennsylvanian, May 10, 2024. www.thedp.com.
33. Robert Cohen, "Opinion: Today's Protests Are Tamer than the Campus Unrest of the 1960s. So Why the Harsh Response?," *Los Angeles Times*, May 14, 2024. www.latimes.com.
34. Quoted in Michael Loria and Christopher Cann, "No Diploma: Colleges Withhold Degrees from Students After Pro-Palestinian Protests," *USA Today*, June 4, 2024. www.usatoday.com.
35. Quoted in Helen Pearson, "The Science of Protests: How to Shape Public Opinion and Swing Votes," *Nature*, June 26, 2024. www.nature.com.
36. Quoted in Pearson, "The Science of Protests."
37. Quoted in Pearson, "The Science of Protests."
38. David French, "Colleges Have Gone off the Deep End. There Is a Way Out," *New York Times*, April 28, 2024. www.nytimes.com.

Chapter Four: Vandalism and Violence on Campus

39. Quoted in Jaysha Patel, "Classes Canceled at UCLA After Night of Violence Between Protest Groups," ABC 7, May 1, 2024. https://abc7.com.
40. Quoted in Elyssa Cherney and Genevieve Bookwalter, "'Disgusted' NU President Condemns Students Who Burned a School Banner and Vandalized Campus During Police Protests, Sparking Calls for His Resignation," *Chicago Tribune*, October 21, 2020. www.chicagotribune.com.
41. Quoted in Cherney and Bookwalter, "'Disgusted' NU President Condemns Students Who Burned a School Banner and Vandalized Campus During Police Protests, Sparking Calls for His Resignation."
42. Quoted in Cherney and Bookwalter, "'Disgusted' NU President Condemns Students Who Burned a School Banner and Vandalized Campus During Police Protests, Sparking Calls for His Resignation."
43. Quoted in Helier Cheung, "George Floyd Death: Why Do Some Protests Turn Violent?," BBC News, May 31, 2020. www.bbc.com.

44. Quoted in Rachel Triesman, "She Survived the 1970 Kent State Shooting. Here's Her Message to Student Activists," NPR, May 4, 2024. www.npr.org.
45. Quoted in Emily Arntsen, "Are Peaceful Protests More Effective than Violent Ones?," Northeastern Global News, June 10, 2020. https://news.northeastern.edu.
46. Quoted in Melissa De Witte, "Violence by Protesters Can Lead the Public to Support Them Less, Stanford Sociologist Says," Stanford Report, October 12, 2018. https://news.stanford.edu.
47. Quoted in Laura Bassett, "Why Violent Protests Work," *GQ*, June 2, 2020. www.gq.com.
48. Quoted in Gabrielle Canon, "The US Universities That Allow Protest Encampments—and Even Negotiate," *The Guardian* (Manchester, UK), May 4, 2024. www.theguardian.com.
49. Quoted in Kristin Bender, "Student Protests: Are They the Best and Most Efficient Way to Spark Social Change?," *Port Huron (MI) Times-Herald*, April 29, 2024. www.timesheraldonline.com.

Chapter Five: The Future of Student Protests

50. Quoted in Pearson, "The Science of Protests."
51. UNICEF Innocenti, *Youth, Protests and the Polycrisis*. Florence, Italy: UNICEF Innocenti, 2024, p. 9. www.unicef.org.
52. Quoted in Rivers et al., "Will the Generational Divide on Support for Israel Impact the Presidential Election?"
53. Quoted in Megan Carnegie, "Gen Z: How Young People Are Changing Activism," BBC, August 8, 2022. www.bbc.com.
54. Quoted in Carnegie, "Gen Z."
55. Quoted in Carnegie, "Gen Z."
56. Quoted in Carnegie, "Gen Z."
57. Quoted in Carnegie, "Gen Z."
58. Quoted in Charla Agnoletti, "Youth-Led Activism Is Key to Building a Better World," Teach for America, January 25, 2021. www.teachforamerica.org.
59. UNICEF Innocenti, *Youth, Protests and the Polycrisis*, p. 25.
60. Quoted in Roby Chavez, "Why Youth Activists in Louisiana Say They'll 'No Longer Stay Quiet,'" *PBS NewsHour*, May 18, 2023. www.pbs.org.
61. Quoted in Carnegie, "Gen Z."

FOR FURTHER RESEARCH

Books

Marty Gitlin, *Student Protests*. New York: Greenhaven, 2020.

Danielle Haynes, *Student Activism: The Courage of Your Convictions*. New York: Rosen, 2023.

Avery Elizabeth Hurt, *The Power of Protest*. New York: Greenhaven, 2023.

Michael G. Long, *Kids on the March: 15 Stories of Speaking Out, Protesting, and Fighting for Justice*. Chapel Hill, NC: Algonquin Young Readers, 2021.

Ian Rosenberg, *Free Speech Handbook: A Practical Framework for Understanding Our Free Speech Protections*. New York: First Second, 2021.

Internet Sources

American Civil Liberties Union, "Open Letter to College and University Presidents on Student Protests," April 26, 2024. www.aclu.org.

Foundation for Individual Rights and Expression, "Here's What Students Need to Know About Protesting on Campus Right Now," April 25, 2024. www.fire.org.

PBS NewsHour, "Campus Protesters Are Violating Rights of Other Students, Argues David French," May 7, 2024. www.pbs.org.

United States Courts, "What Does Free Speech Mean?" www.uscourts.gov.

Organizations and Websites

American Civil Liberties Union (ACLU)
www.aclu.org
The ACLU is a nonprofit organization that works to defend and preserve the individual rights and liberties guaranteed to every citizen by the Constitution and US laws. Its website provides information about freedom of speech.

Black Lives Matter (BLM)
https://blacklivesmatter.com
BLM is a political and social movement that works to highlight racism, discrimination, and racial inequality and promote antiracism. Its website provides the latest news and resources on racial issues.

Foundation for Individual Rights and Expression (FIRE)
www.thefire.org
FIRE works to defend the individual rights of all Americans to free speech and free thought. Its website provides the latest research, news, and information about free speech.

Free Speech Center
https://firstamendment.mtsu.edu
The Free Speech Center at Middle Tennessee State University is a nonprofit public policy center dedicated to promoting education, information sharing, and engagement concerning the First Amendment. Its website has articles, news, and other information related to the First Amendment.

Fridays for Future
https://fridaysforfuture.org
Fridays for Future is an international, student-led movement that protests the lack of action on earth's climate crisis. Its website has information on getting involved in local climate strikes and links to social media feeds for local chapters worldwide.

March for Our Lives
https://marchforourlives.org
March for Our Lives is a student-led organization that leads demonstrations in support of gun control legislation. Its website has information and news about gun control issues, protest activities, and more.

National Constitution Center
https://constitutioncenter.org
The National Constitution Center is the leading platform for constitutional education. Its website provides the full text of the Constitution and its amendments, as well as a library of Supreme Court cases concerning constitutional issues.

INDEX

Note: Boldface page numbers indicate illustrations.

Acuna, Victoria, 54
Adams, Eric, 5, 31–32
Ajmera, Ishan Bipin, 24
Alger, Jonathan, 20
Alverez, Erika, 26
American Civil Liberties Union (ACLU), 61
anti-apartheid protests, 26
anti-Semitism, 31

Barnard College, 29
Biden, Joe, 22
Bipartisan Safer Communities Act (2022), 22–23
Black Lives Matter (BLM), 25–26, 49, **49**, 62
  impacts of, 35
Boston Tea Party (1773), 11
Brown, Michael, 18
Brown University, 45–46

Callaway, Will, 14
Canfora, Alan, 43
Canfora, Roseann, 43
Cavalier, Rebecca, 55
Chabad (Jewish organization), 6
Change Is Brewing campaign, 54
civil disobedience, 11
civil rights movement, 7
  lunch counter sit-ins and, 12–13
climate activism, 14, 23–25, 56
Clock Tower Accords (Saint Louis University), 18
Cohen, Robert, 15, 34
Columbia University
  Jewish students at, **32**
  protests against Israel-Hamas War at, 4–7, **5**, 30, 31–32
Comprehensive Anti-Apartheid Act (1986), 26

Constitution, US
  signing of, **9**
  See also First Amendment
Corin, Jaclyn, 20–21
crowdfunding websites, 53
Cruz, Nikolas, 20

Dartmouth College, 47
Discord (chat room platform), 52
diversity, equity, and inclusion (DEI), protests to promote, 26–27
Duncan, Kyle, 31

Earth Day, 14
Extinction Rebellion Youth, 56

Fall, Natalie, 23
Fenves, Gregory, 41
First Amendment, 8–9, 28
  applications to public vs. private colleges, 10–11
  student protests uphold freedoms of, 17
Floyd, George, 20, 25
Foundation for Individual Rights and Expression (FIRE), 62
Freedom Forum, 10
Freedom's Orator (Cohen), 15
free expression, right to, 9
  limits on, 9–10
Free Speech Center, 62
Free Speech Movement (FSM), 14–15
French, David, 37
Fridays for Future, 62
#FridaysforFuture, 23
Fritz, Livia, 25
fundraising, 53

Gallatin, Amy, 29
Gaza Solidarity Encampment (Columbia University), **5**
Gillion, Daniel, 44

Goldberg, Kevin, 10
Great Depression, student activism during, 12
gun reform protests, 20–23, 52

Harris, LaTesha, 40–41
Hasweh, Youssef, 35
Haworth, Ian, 31

Israel-Hamas War protests, 28–29
  anti-Semitism and, 6, 31–32
  clash between demonstrators in, 38–39, **39**
  at Columbia University, 4–7, **5**
  conflict between protesters'/students' rights in, 28–29
  at Emory University, 41
  potential consequences of, 35
  at Stanford University, 45

James Madison University, 20
Jewish students
  at Columbia University, **32**
  harassment of, 6–7, 31–32
Johnson, F. Willis, Jr., 17
Joshi, Elise, 54

Kasky, Cameron, 20–21
Keme, Emil', 41
Kent State University shooting (1970), 16, **42**, 42–43, 44–45
King, Martin Luther, Jr., 12–13

Larive, Cynthia, 29
Lawrence, Frederick, 28
LGBTQ+ rights activism, 55
lunch counter sit-ins, 12–13, **13**
Lyons, Daerenz, 20

63

March for Our Lives, 20, 21–23, **22**, 53, 62
Marjory Stoneman Douglas High School shooting (Parkland, FL, 2018), 20
Martin, Trayvon, 25
McKenzie-Jackson, Elijah, 52–53, **55**, 55–56
Mintz, Steven, 23
Mueller, Lisa, 36, 48
Myers, VonDerrit, Jr., 18

National Constitution Center, 62
Nelson, Gaylord, 14
news, teens' sources of, 50–51
Nixon, Richard, 42, 45
nonviolence
　in civil disobedience, 11
　impact of protests and, 36, 44
　in lunch counter sit-ins, 13
　in student protests, 19–20
Northwestern University, 40–41

October 7 Hamas attack (2023), 4
online protests, 53
opinion polls. *See* surveys
Osako, Mary, 39

Paxson, Christina, 45–46
Perrino, Nico, 31
Pestello, Fred, 18–19
Pew Research Center, 53
police brutality, protests against, 25–26
　See also Black Lives Matter
　at Northwestern University, 40–41
polls. *See* surveys
Project on Security and Threats (University of Chicago), 31
protest movements
　ebb and flows in, 49
　effectiveness of, 8, 25–27, 35–37
　global online, 52–54
　growth in, 48

growth in youth participation in, 54–56
raise visibility of issues, 7
public opinion
　impact of Kent State University shooting, 42–43
　impact of protests on, 7, 36, 43–45
　See also surveys

Rabrenovic, Gordana, 43–44
Radey, Jack, 47
Roosevelt, Franklin D., 12

Saint Louis University, 18–19
　protest at, **19**
Schapiro, Morton, 40
Schill, Michael, 33
school shootings, protests against, 20–21
School Strike for Climate, 53
Shafik, Minouche, 5
Shapiro, Robert, 7
Shuman, Eric, 37
Singer, Peter, 11
Sinha, Subir, 50, 52
Slater, Samantha, 6–7
Stone, Geoffrey, 10
Stott, Clifford, 41–42
Student Nonviolent Coordinating Committee, 13
student protests
　approaches to preventing violence in, 45–47
　arising from grassroots efforts, 20–21
　civil disobedience and, 11
　for civil rights, 12–13
　debate over use of police to break up, 34
　disciplinary actions against participant in, 35
　history of, in US, 7, 11–12
　importance of police response to, 41–43
　for increased diversity, 26
　against Israel-Hamas War, 4–6, 28–29

limitations on, 10–11
schools' responsibilities/responses to, 32–34
silencing controversial speakers, 31
tactics of, 16–17
uphold First Amendment freedoms, 17
use of violence/vandalism in, 40–41
surveys
　on social media and awareness of issues, 53
　on teens' sources of news, 50–51
Swart, Adam, 45
Swiss Federal Institute of Technology Lausanne, 25

Taft, Jessica, 49–50
teach-ins, 14, 15–16, 18
Thunberg, Greta, 23–24, **24**
Tovar, Liz, 27

UNICEF, 48
University of California, Berkeley, Free Speech Movement begins at, 14–15
University of California, Los Angeles (UCLA), 38, **39**
University of California, Santa Cruz, 28–29
University of Chicago, 31
University of Iowa, 26–27
University of Michigan, 15
University of Pennsylvania, 33–34, 46–47
　encampment at, **46**
　protester detained at, **34**
University of Southern California, 30

Vietnam War, origins of, 15
Vietnam War protests, 7, 15–16, **16**
Volokh, Eugene, 10

Washington, George, **9**
Wasow, Omar, 30, 36, 49
Willer, Robb, 44
Wind, Alex, 20–21
Wizner, Ben, 10–11